NEIL DIAMOND

THE GREATEST HITS

1966-1992

Hal Leonard Publishing Corporation

7777 West Bluemound Road P.O. Box 13819 Milwaukee, WI 53213

ISBN 0-7935-1433-9

ART DIRECTION & DESIGN: **DAVID KIRSCHNER**   ADDITIONAL DESIGN: **JAN WEINBERG**
(ADAPTED FROM THE COMPACT DISC)

SOLITARY MAN

Words and Music by
NEIL DIAMOND

CHERRY, CHERRY

Words and Music by
NEIL DIAMOND

To Coda

Tell your ma - ma, girl, ___ I can't stay long.
No, we won't ___ tell a soul ___ where we gone to.

We got things ___ we got ___ to catch
Girl, we got do ___ what - ev - er we

up on.
want to.

Ah, you know, ___
Ah, I love ___

I GOT THE FEELIN'
(OH NO, NO)

Words and Music by
NEIL DIAMOND

GIRL, YOU'LL BE A WOMAN SOON

Words and Music by
NEIL DIAMOND

Love you so much, can't count all the ways I'd die for you girl; and all they can say is,

"He's not your kind." They

nev - er get tired of put - tin' me down, and I nev - er know when I come a - round

THANK THE LORD FOR THE NIGHT TIME

Words and Music by
NEIL DIAMOND

KENTUCKY WOMAN

Words and Music by
NEIL DIAMOND

Ken-tuck - y wom -
Well, she ain't the kind

- an, she shines with her own kind of light.
makes heads turn at the drop of her name.

She'd look at you once, and a day that's all wrong looks all right.
But some-thing in - side that she's got turns you on just the same.

SHILO

Words and Music by
NEIL DIAMOND

YOU GOT TO ME

Words and Music by
NEIL DIAMOND

38

BROOKLYN ROADS

Words and Music by
NEIL DIAMOND

44

CRACKLIN' ROSIE

Words and Music by
NEIL DIAMOND

Crack-lin' Ros-ie, get on board.

We're gon-na ride till there ain't no more to go, tak-in' it slow.

And Lord don't you know I'll

hang on to me,__ girl, our song__ keeps run - nin' on._____

no chord

Play it now!__ Play it now!__

1.

Play it now,__ my ba - by! Play it now,__ my ba - by!

2.

Crack - lin' Ros - ie, make me smile.__ And girl, if it lasts__ for an hour,__

RED, RED WINE

Words and Music by
NEIL DIAMOND

I'M A BELIEVER

Words and Music by
NEIL DIAMOND

SWEET CAROLINE

Words and Music by
NEIL DIAMOND

SOOLAIMON

Words and Music by
NEIL DIAMOND

SONG SUNG BLUE

Words and Music by
NEIL DIAMOND

and be-fore you know it start to feel-in' good. __ You sim-ply got no choice. __

Fun - ny thing, __ but you can sing _____ it with a

cry in your voice __ and be-fore you know it start to feel-in' good. __

You sim - ply got no choice. __

D.S. al Coda

CODA

PLAY ME

Words and Music by
NEIL DIAMOND

HOLLY HOLY

Words and Music by
NEIL DIAMOND

CRUNCHY GRANOLA SUITE

Words and Music by
NEIL DIAMOND

Drop your shrink __ and stop __ your drink - in'; crunch - y gran - o - la's neat! __

Sing it out, __

all

right.

MORNINGSIDE
(FOR MY CHILDREN)

Words and Music by
NEIL DIAMOND

BROTHER LOVE'S TRAVELING SALVATION SHOW

Words and Music by
NEIL DIAMOND

LONGFELLOW SERENADE

Words and Music by
NEIL DIAMOND

Long - fel - low Se - re - nade.
Long - fel - low Se - re - nade.

Such were the plans I'd made. For
Such were the plans I made. But

she was a la - dy, and I was a dream-er with on - ly words to trade.
she was a la - dy as deep as the ri - ver, and through the night we stayed.

I AM...I SAID

Words and Music by
NEIL DIAMOND

L. A.'s fine, __ the sun shines most the time

and the feel-in' is lay back.

Palm trees grow and rents are low, __ but you know I keep think-in' 'bout __

BE

(from "JONATHAN LIVINGSTON SEAGULL", the film by Hall Bartlett)

Words and Music by
NEIL DIAMOND

122

one God will make for ___ your way.

To Coda

gat the spark,___ turned to liv-ing bone.___ Ho-ly, ho-ly.

D.S. al Coda

Sanc - tus,___ sanc - tus.___

CODA

BEAUTIFUL NOISE

Words and Music by
NEIL DIAMOND

IF YOU KNOW WHAT I MEAN

Words and Music by
NEIL DIAMOND

DESIRÉE

Words and Music by
NEIL DIAMOND

Moderate Rock beat

It was the   third of June
fourth of June

on that young - er   day.
on that sleep - less night.

Well, I be -
Well, I

SEPTEMBER MORN

Words and Music by NEIL DIAMOND
and GILBERT BECAUD

YOU DON'T BRING ME FLOWERS

Words by NEIL DIAMOND,
MARILYN BERGMAN, ALAN BERGMAN
Music by NEIL DIAMOND

150

FOREVER IN BLUE JEANS

Words and Music by NEIL DIAMOND
and RICHARD BENNETT

HELLO AGAIN

(from the motion picture "THE JAZZ SINGER")

Words by NEIL DIAMOND
Music by NEIL DIAMOND and ALAN LINDGREN

AMERICA
(from the motion picture "THE JAZZ SINGER")

Words and Music by
NEIL DIAMOND

LOVE ON THE ROCKS

Words and Music by NEIL DIAMOND
and GILBERT BECAUD

Moderately slow ballad

Love on the rocks

ain't no sur-prise.

Pour me a drink, __ and I'll

tell you some lies. __

Got noth-in' to lose, __ so you

YESTERDAY'S SONGS

Words and Music by
NEIL DIAMOND

HEARTLIGHT

Words and Music by NEIL DIAMOND,
BURT BACHARACH and CAROLE BAYER SAGER

HEADED FOR THE FUTURE

Words by NEIL DIAMOND
Music by NEIL DIAMOND, TOM HENSLEY and ALAN LINDGREN

now.

Show you ___ how. _

HEARTBREAK HOTEL

By MAE BOREN AXTON,
TOMMY DURDEN and ELVIS PRESLEY

Moderate Shuffle

Well, since my __ ba - by left me, well I found a new place to dwell. Well, it's

down at the end __ of Lone - ly Street, that's Heart - break Ho - tel. where I'll be...

I'll be so lone - ly, ba - by. Well, I'm so lone - ly.

ALL I REALLY NEED IS YOU

Words by NEIL DIAMOND
Music by NEIL DIAMOND, ALAN LINDGREN and TOM HENSLEY